2 Describe fully each of the numbered melodic intervals (e.g. major 2nd).

Nielsen, *Commotio*

Reproduced by permission of Chester Music Ltd.

Intervals:

1. ....

2. ....

3. ....

4. ....

5. ....

3 The following melody is written for clarinet in B♭. Transpose it down a major 2nd, as it will sound at concert pitch. Remember to put in the new key signature.

Elgar, *Cockaigne*

© Copyright 1901 by Boosey & Co. Ltd.
Reproduced by permission of Boosey & Hawkes Music Publishers Ltd.

4 Look at this extract and then answer the questions on page 5.

SCHERZO
Allegro vivace con delicatezza

Schubert, Piano Sonata in B♭ D. 960

The Associated Board of
the Royal Schools of Music

Theory of

Music

Examinations

GRADE 5

1999

Theory Paper Grade 5   1999   A

Duration 2 hours

This paper contains SEVEN questions, ALL of which should be answered.
Write your answers on this paper — no others will be accepted.
Answers must be written clearly and neatly — otherwise marks may be lost.

TOTAL MARKS
100

1 (a) (i)   Add the time signature to this extract, which begins on the first beat of the bar.

10

Britten, *Peter Grimes*

(ii)   Write suitable rests at ✳ to complete the bar.

(b) (i)   Describe the chords marked **A** and **B** in the extract below as I, II, IV or V.
Also indicate whether the root, 3rd or 5th is in the bass. The key is D major.

A ....   **B** ....

(ii)   Below the staves write $\begin{smallmatrix}6\\4\end{smallmatrix}\begin{smallmatrix}5\\3\end{smallmatrix}$ (Ic–V) under the two chords where this progression occurs.

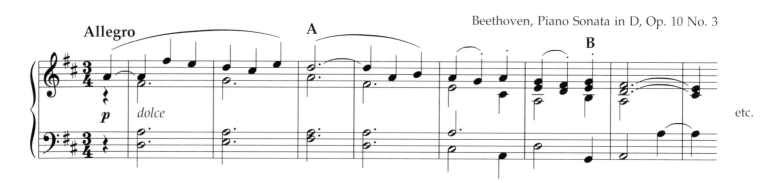

Beethoven, Piano Sonata in D, Op. 10 No. 3

(a) (i) Give the meaning of: [10]

SCHERZO ....

Allegro vivace ....

8------ (bars 7–8) ....

(ii) Write an enharmonic equivalent of the first right-hand note of bar 5.

(iii) Name the ornament in the right hand of bar 7. ....

(b) (i) Compare bars 1–8 with bars 9–16. Name two similarities and two differences. [10]

Similarities 1. ....

2. ....

Differences 1. ....

2. ....

(ii) From the beginning to bar 12 the music is in the key of B♭ major. Within these bars draw a circle round a right-hand submediant note and a left-hand leading note in this key.

(iii) In what key is the music at bar 16? ....

(c) (i) Write the first left-hand note of bar 9 so that it sounds the same, but using the tenor clef. [10]

(ii) Write the last left-hand note of bar 13 so that it sounds the same, but using the alto clef.

(iii) Name a standard orchestral string instrument which uses the alto clef. ....

(iv) Name a standard orchestral woodwind instrument which sometimes uses the tenor clef.

....

(v) Name a standard orchestral brass instrument which could play the left-hand part of bars 9–14.

....

5

5 (a) Write the **ascending** melodic minor scale which has the given key signature.
Use semibreves (whole notes).

(b) Put sharps or flats in front of the notes which need them to form the scale of F♯ major.
Do *not* use a key signature.

6 EITHER

(a) Compose a melody for violin, oboe or trumpet, using the given opening. Indicate the tempo and other performance directions, including any which might be particularly required for the instrument chosen. The complete melody should not be more than eight bars long.

Instrument for which the melody is written. ....

OR

(b) Compose a melody for the following words. Write each syllable under the note or notes to which it is to be sung. Also indicate the tempo and other performance directions as appropriate.

> Ann, Ann! Come! quick as you can!
> There's a fish that *talks* in the frying-pan.
>
> *Walter de la Mare*

7 Suggest suitable progressions for two cadences in the following melody by indicating one chord (I, II, IV or V) at each of the places marked A – E. You do not have to indicate the position of the chords, or to state which note is in the bass.

Show the chords:

EITHER (a) by writing notes on the staves;

OR (b) by writing I, II etc. or any other recognised symbols on the dotted lines below.

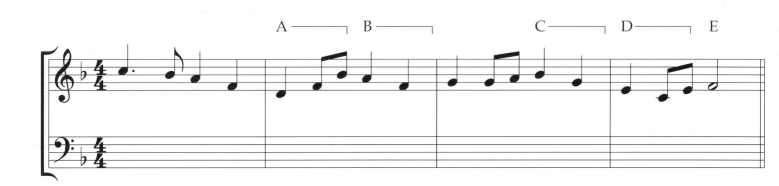

FIRST CADENCE:

Chord A ....

Chord B ....

SECOND CADENCE:

Chord C ....

Chord D ....

Chord E ....

BLANK PAGE

Theory Paper Grade 5 1999 B

Duration 2 hours

This paper contains SEVEN questions, ALL of which should be answered.
Write your answers on this paper — no others will be accepted.
Answers must be written clearly and neatly — otherwise marks may be lost.

TOTAL MARKS
100

1 (a) (i)   Add the time signature to this extract, which begins on the first beat of the bar.

J. S. Bach, *Es wartet alles auf dich*

(ii) Write suitable rests to complete the final bar.

(iii) Describe fully the melodic interval marked ☐. ....

(b) This passage begins on the first beat of the bar and contains some changes of time.
    Put in the time signature at the beginning and elsewhere as necessary.

Christopher Brown, *Pastorale*

2 This passage is for SATB chorus, written in short score. Write it out in open score.

Bennet, *Weep, O mine eyes*

etc.

3 Look at this extract and then answer the questions on page 13.

Look at this extract and then answer the questions on page 13.

Mozart, Violin Sonata in G, K. 379

Andantino cantabile

Violin

Piano

(a) (i) Give the meaning of **Andantino cantabile**.

....

(ii) Describe fully the melodic intervals marked **1**, **2** and **3**.

1 (bar 2, piano, left hand) ....

2 (bar 6, piano, left hand) ....

3 (bar 10, violin)   ....

10

(b) (i) Describe each of the chords marked **A**, **B** and **C** as I, II, IV or V. Also indicate whether the root, 3rd or 5th is in the bass. The key is G major.

Chord **A** (bar 5)   ....

Chord **B** (bar 13)   ....

Chord **C** (bar 16)   ....

10

(ii) Complete the following statement:

The extract begins and ends in the key of G major. At bar 8 it reaches the key

of .... , and is in the key of A minor during bar ....

(c) (i) Write out bar 8 of the violin part so that it sounds the same, but using the tenor clef.

10

(ii) Name a standard orchestral brass instrument which sometimes uses the tenor clef.

....

(iii) Name two standard orchestral instruments, one woodwind and one brass, which could play bars 13–16 of the violin part **an octave lower**.

Woodwind   ....

Brass   ....

4 **(i)** Put any necessary sharps or flats in front of the notes which need them to form the scale of B♭ melodic minor ascending. Do *not* use a key signature.

(ii) Give the technical names (tonic, dominant etc.) of the notes marked **A** and **B**.

A ....

B ....

(iii) Write an enharmonic equivalent of the first note of the scale.

5 The notes below are those actually sounded by a horn in F. Write them out as they would be printed for the player to read. The transposition is a perfect 5th up. Do not use a key signature but remember to put in all necessary accidentals.

Bloch, *Schelomo*

Reproduced by permission of G. Schirmer Ltd
on behalf of G. Schirmer, Inc.

6 EITHER

(a) Compose a melody for cello, bassoon or trombone, using the given opening. Indicate the tempo and other performance directions, including any which might be particularly required for the instrument chosen. The complete melody should not be more than eight bars long.

Instrument for which the melody is written. ....

OR

(b) Compose a melody for the following words. Write each syllable under the note or notes to which it is to be sung. Also indicate the tempo and other performance directions as appropriate.

> The shadows now so long do grow
> That brambles like tall cedars show.
>
> *Charles Cotton*

7 Suggest suitable progressions for two cadences in the following melody by indicating
one chord (I, II, IV or V) at each of the places marked A – E. You do not have to indicate
the position of the chords, or to state which note is in the bass.

Show the chords:

EITHER   (a)   by writing notes on the staves;

OR   (b)   by writing I, II etc. or any other recognised symbols on the dotted lines below.

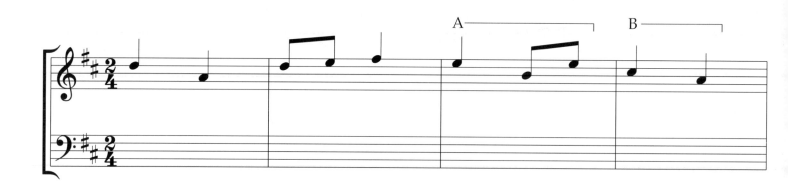

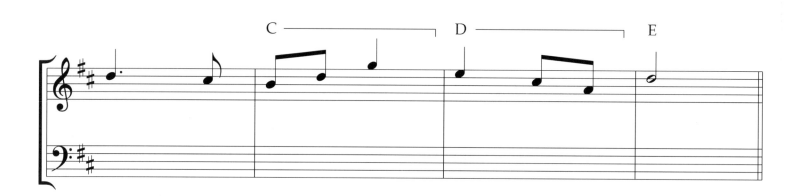

FIRST CADENCE: SECOND CADENCE:

Chord C ....

Chord A ....

Chord D ....

Chord B ....

Chord E ....

BLANK PAGE

Theory Paper Grade 5   1999   C

Duration 2 hours

This paper contains SEVEN questions, ALL of which should be answered.
Write your answers on this paper — no others will be accepted.
Answers must be written clearly and neatly — otherwise marks may be lost.

TOTAL MARKS
100

1 (a) In this extract several changes of time signature are needed. Put the time signatures
in the appropriate places.

Peter Maxwell Davies, *Winterfold*

Reproduced by permission of Chester Music Ltd.

(b) Add appropriate rests at ∗ to complete the bar.

2 Describe fully each of the numbered melodic intervals (e.g. major 2nd).

Strauss, *Der Rosenkavalier*

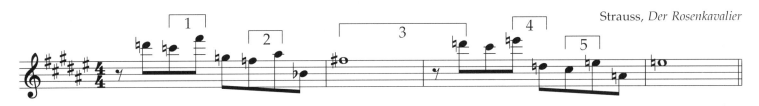

Intervals:

1. ....

2. ....

3. ....

4. ....

5. ....

3 This passage is written for a clarinet in A. Transpose it down a minor 3rd, as it will  sound at concert pitch. Remember to put in the new key signature.

Wagner, *Das Rheingold*

4 (i) Write in semibreves (whole notes) the **descending** scale of E♭ harmonic minor. Do  *not* use a key signature but put in all necessary sharps or flats. The first note of the scale is given.

(ii) Write the key signature of five sharps after the following clef and then one octave, **ascending**, of the major scale which has this key signature. Use semibreves (whole notes).

5 Look at this extract and then answer the questions on page 21.

Presto, ma non troppo

Haydn, Piano Sonata in D, Hob. XVI/37

(a) (i) Give the meaning of:

       Presto, ma non troppo ....

       ᵥ (right hand, e.g. bar 2) ....

    (ii) Name the ornaments used in bars 6 and 7.

       Bar 6 ....

       Bar 7 ....

10

(b) (i) Describe each of the chords marked **A**, **B** and **C** as I, II, IV or V. Also indicate whether the root, 3rd or 5th is in the bass. Regard the key as D major throughout.

       Chord **A** (bar 7) ....

       Chord **B** (bar 10) ....

       Chord **C** (bar 18) ....

10

    (ii) Write out bar 1 of the left-hand part so that it sounds the same, but using the tenor clef.

    (iii) Write an enharmonic equivalent of the last right-hand note of bar 5.

(c) (i) Compare bars 1–4 with bars 13–16. Name one similarity and two differences that you notice.

       Similarity   ....

       Difference 1   ....

       Difference 2   ....

10

    (ii) Name a standard orchestral instrument which could play the first eight bars of the right-hand part **an octave lower** and name the family to which it belongs.

       Instrument ....   Family ....

(a) Compose a melody for violin or flute, using the given minuet-style opening. Indicate the tempo and other performance directions, including any which might be particularly required for the instrument chosen. The complete melody should not be more than eight bars long.

Instrument for which the melody is written. ....

OR

(b) Compose a melody for the following words. Write each syllable under the note or notes to which it is to be sung. Also indicate the tempo and other performance directions as appropriate.

> All in the town were still asleep
> When the sun came up with a shout and a leap. *Rupert Brooke*

7 Suggest suitable progressions for two cadences in the following melody by indicating [15] one chord (I, II, IV or V) at each of the places marked A – E. You do not have to indicate the position of the chords, or to state which note is in the bass.

Show the chords:

EITHER   (a) by writing notes on the staves;

OR   (b) by writing I, II etc. or any other recognised symbols on the dotted lines below.

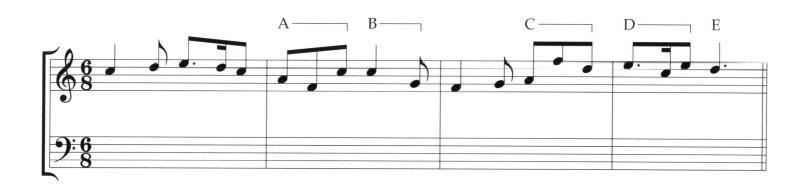

FIRST CADENCE:

Chord A   ....

Chord B   ....

SECOND CADENCE:

Chord C   ....

Chord D   ....

Chord E   ....

Theory Paper Grade 5   1999   S

Duration 2 hours

This paper contains SEVEN questions, ALL of which should be answered.
Write your answers on this paper — no others will be accepted.
Answers must be written clearly and neatly — otherwise marks may be lost.

TOTAL MARKS
100

1 This extract begins on the first beat of the bar and has a number of changes of time
   signature. Put in the time signature at the beginning and elsewhere, as necessary.

Howells, *Antiphon*

© Oxford University Press 1978. Reproduced by permission.

2 This passage is as written for clarinet in B♭. Transpose it down a major 2nd, as it will
   sound at concert pitch. Remember to put in the new key signature.

Franck, Symphony in D

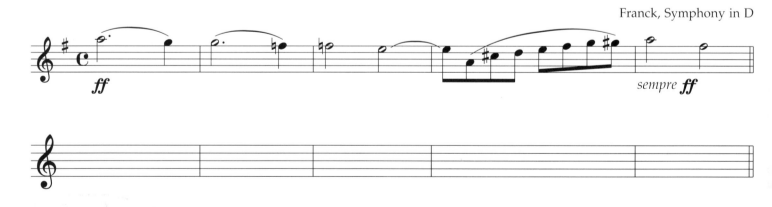

3 Rewrite the following in short score.

Bruckner, *Tota pulchra es*

4 This is part of an aria from Mozart's opera, *The Marriage of Figaro,* with the orchestral part arranged for piano. Look at it and then answer the questions on page 27.

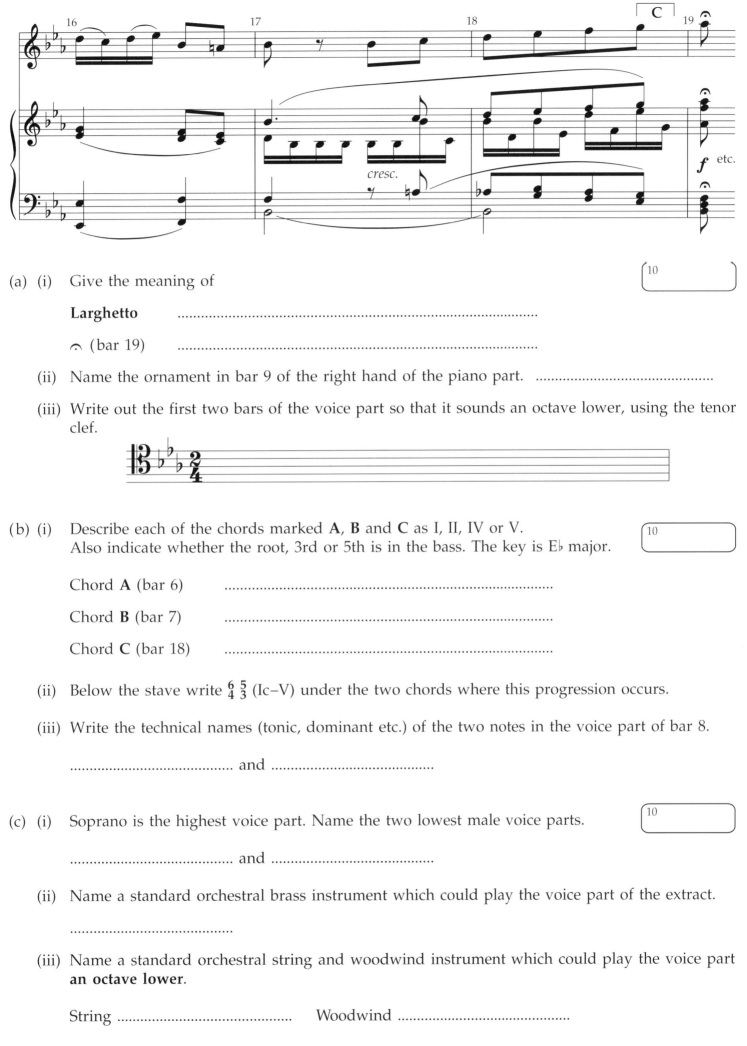

(a) (i) Give the meaning of

    Larghetto ....

    ⌢ (bar 19) ....

(ii) Name the ornament in bar 9 of the right hand of the piano part. ....

(iii) Write out the first two bars of the voice part so that it sounds an octave lower, using the tenor clef.

(b) (i) Describe each of the chords marked **A**, **B** and **C** as I, II, IV or V.
Also indicate whether the root, 3rd or 5th is in the bass. The key is E♭ major.

    Chord **A** (bar 6) ....

    Chord **B** (bar 7) ....

    Chord **C** (bar 18) ....

(ii) Below the stave write $^6_4$ $^5_3$ (Ic–V) under the two chords where this progression occurs.

(iii) Write the technical names (tonic, dominant etc.) of the two notes in the voice part of bar 8.

    .... and ....

(c) (i) Soprano is the highest voice part. Name the two lowest male voice parts.

    .... and ....

(ii) Name a standard orchestral brass instrument which could play the voice part of the extract.

    ....

(iii) Name a standard orchestral string and woodwind instrument which could play the voice part **an octave lower**.

    String ....   Woodwind ....

5 (a) After the following clef write the key signature and put in any sharps or flats needed  to form the scale of G♯ melodic minor ascending.

(b) Describe fully the numbered melodic intervals (e.g. major 2nd).

Beethoven, *Grosse Fuge*, Op. 133

Intervals:

1. ....

2. ....

(a) Compose a melody for violin, oboe or horn, using the given opening. Indicate the tempo and other performance directions, including any which might be particularly required for the instrument chosen. The complete melody should not be more than eight bars long.

Instrument for which the melody is written. ....

OR

(b) Compose a melody for the following words. Write each syllable under the note or notes to which it is to be sung. Also indicate the tempo and other performance directions as appropriate.

> Reindeer are coming to drive you away
> Over the snow on an ebony sleigh.
>
> *W. H. Auden*

Text reproduced by permission of Curtis Brown Ltd, London, on behalf of the Estate of W. H. Auden. Copyright W. H. Auden and Christopher Isherwood.

7 Suggest suitable progressions for two cadences in the following melody by indicating one chord (I, II, IV or V) at each of the places marked A – E. You do not have to indicate the position of the chords, or to state which note is in the bass.

Show the chords:

EITHER   (a) by writing notes on the staves;

OR   (b) by writing I, II etc. or any other recognised symbols on the dotted lines below.

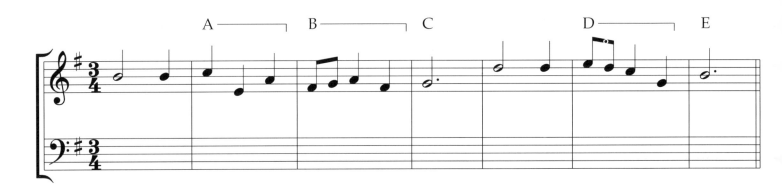

FIRST CADENCE:

Chord A ....

Chord B ....

Chord C ....

SECOND CADENCE:

Chord D ....

Chord E ....

ABRSM
PUBLISHING

**The Associated Board of
the Royal Schools of Music
(Publishing) Limited**

14 Bedford Square
London WC1B 3JG
United Kingdom

www.abrsmpublishing.co.uk

ISBN 1-86096-079-0

The Associated Board of the Royal Schools of Music

Theory of

Music

Examinations

GRADE 4

1996

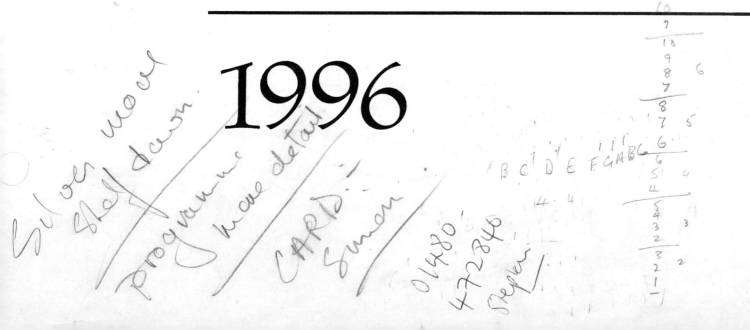

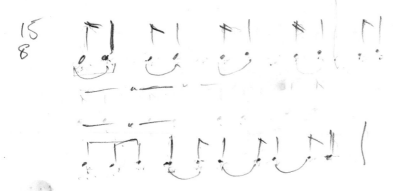

and ev-er to sing from no-on to noon

Two ~~Red Ro-ses~~
Red Ro——ses ~~de-nos~~
a-cross the moon